AN INQUIRY

INTO THE

CAUSES OF THE PRESENT LONG-CONTINUED DEPRESSION IN THE COTTON TRADE;

WITH

SUGGESTIONS FOR ITS IMPROVEMENT.

BY

A COTTON MANUFACTURER.

MANCHESTER: JOHN HEYWOOD, 143, DEANSGATE.
BURY: LAMBERT FLETCHER.

1869.

[PRICE TWOPENCE.]

PREFACE.

The writer of this pamphlet, being himself very extensively engaged in business as a Spinner and Manufacturer, has naturally had his attention drawn to the seriously depressed condition of our trade and commerce; and also to the various plans which have been propounded for their improvement.

Without offering any opinion as to the value of any of these schemes, he yet ventures to express an opinion, that unless the suggestions offered in the following pages be attended to, there can never be any sound or lasting improvement in the Cotton Trade of this country. The writer wishes further to say, that although the argument in the tract is applied to the Cotton Trade, yet the thoughtful reader will see that it will equally, if not to the same extent, apply to all other departments of our national industry.

W. H.

AN INQUIRY

INTO THE

CAUSES OF THE PRESENT LONG-CONTINUED DEPRESSION IN THE COTTON TRADE.

FOR many years, indeed ever since the American War, the cotton trade has been a very precarious and unprofitable one. Whilst the war lasted this was cheerfully borne, in hopes that when it ended increased prosperity would return, but since the conclusion of the war things have been worse than ever; spinners and manufacturers are spinning away their money; on 'Change men begin to look dejected; mills are being locked up, and sold for one-third their cost. What is to be done? is the question daily asked, but as yet the answer comes not. I believe the remedy lies entirely with ourselves.

There is a very general and growing impression that the cotton trade in this country has had its day. There have been so many mills started, it is said, on the continent, that little or no cloth is needed from us; indeed, it is often said that large quantities of cloth find their way from Belgium, France, Holland, &c., to London and Manchester; and the prevalent notion is, not only that our trade with continental and other countries is falling off, but that they are beating us in our own markets, and that we who have our property in cotton mills, had better prepare to get quit of them as soon and as best we can.

This is the sort of talk which has been often heard

on the Manchester Exchange for many months back. How does the matter stand? To test this I will take the three years immediately before the American war—viz., 1859, 1860, and 1861. These were three of the best years the cotton trade ever had; and the export of cotton goods during these years was the largest on record. If we compare them with 1866, 1867, and 1868, we get the following results:—

Exports of Cotton Manufactures of all Descriptions.

Year	Yards.	Year	Yards.
1859	2,562,545,476	1866	2,575,698,138
1860	2,776,218,427	1867	2,832,023,707
1861	2,563,459,007	1868	2,966,706,542
	7,902,222,910		8,374,428,387

Showing an increase in the quantity of cotton goods exported in 1866, 1867, and 1868, of 472,205,477 yards over the years 1859, 1860, and 1861.

These figures entirely disprove the notion generally entertained, as to the falling off of our foreign trade; and it will be clear to all, that if our general trade has become worse, and our foreign trade better, our present bad trade must arise from a falling off in the home demand.

It is generally thought by Lancashire merchants and manufacturers, that what little trade we have left owes its continuance mainly to the enormous development of our trade to India, and to the expansion of our home trade; and that not only are the continental markets well nigh supplied without us, but it is generally thought that these countries are actually competing with us in our own markets in the United Kingdom. How far this is correct will be seen from the following tables, which for comparison I have calculated in weight. Contrast our imports and exports to the continent for the years 1859, 1860, and 1861, and 1866, 1867, and 1868 (as the figures for Belgium for 1868 are not yet out, I have taken 1865, 1866, and 1867):—

Exports.

	1859-60-61.		1866-67-68.	
France	12,247,289	lbs.	37,590,056	lbs.
Holland	128,841,125	„	118,537,368	„
Hânse Towns....	142,362,588	„	138,229,899	„
Belgium............	4,824,796	„	11,572,922	„
	288,275,798	„	305,930,245	„

Imports.

(Statistics for 1868 not yet out.)

	1859-60-61.		1865-66-67.	
France	12,531,362	lbs.	13,525,648	lbs.
Holland	8,124,268	„	9,291,879	„
Hanse Towns	5,149,340	„	3,219,754	„
Belgium	3,167,788	„	2,228,385	„
	28,972,758	„	28,265,666	„

From the above tables, which include yarns as well as goods, it will be seen that our entire exports to those countries on the continent which are generally thought to be outstripping us, have increased 6 per cent, and that our imports from them have decreased 2½ per cent.

If we take the exports of cotton cloth merely, we shall find there is a great increase. The following tables will show this:—

Table of Exports.

	1859-60-61.		1866-67-68.	
France	51,704,349	yds.	136,084,895	yds.
Holland	107,657,305	„	120,825,592	„
Hanse Towns....	182,335,175	„	228,764,090	„
Belgium...........	12,485,426	„	29,045,759	„
	354,182,255	„	514,720,336	„

Showing a total increase in our exports of cotton cloth of 160,538,081 yards, or about 45 per cent.

The increase in value is still greater, as the following tables will show:—

TABLE OF EXPORTS.

	1859-60-61.	1866-67-68.
France	£1,130,683	£4,535,759
Holland	7,919,568	12,128,982
Hanse Towns	8,653,487	16,149,849
Belgium	389,815	1,439,826
	£18,093,553	£34,254,416

Showing an increase in value of £16,160,863, or nearly 90 per cent.

Our exports to India for the same three years are as follows:—

1859....886,604,546	yds.	1866....545,404,082	yds.
1860....722,828,446	"	1867....645,885,222	"
1861....735,549,267	"	1868....842,410,665	"
2,344,982,259	"	2,033,699,969	"

A decrease of 311,282,290 yards, or 13 per cent., and if yarns had been included, the decrease would have been still greater.

In the home trade there are not the same statistical returns published as in the export trade, nevertheless our home consumption of cotton goods may be calculated with sufficient nicety to be reliable. To come at this, we have first the amount of cotton taken by the trade; then we have the published tables of exports of goods, and deducting the exports from the cotton used will give us the home consumption.

Mr. Elijah Helm, a friend of mine, in a paper read before the Manchester Statistical Society, and which has been published, has gone into these calculations elaborately. I have had an opportunity of testing his figures by those of other eminent authorities, and find them thoroughly reliable.

He has kindly given me a copy of his paper, from which I extract the following tables:—

ESTIMATED WEIGHT OF COTTON CONTAINED IN MANUFACTURES OF ALL KINDS EXPORTED AND RETAINED FOR HOME CONSUMPTION.

	Weight of cotton consumed after cleaning.		Weight of cleaned cotton in yarn and cloth exported.		Weight of cleaned cotton in goods for home consumption.
	Lbs.		Lbs.		Lbs.
1859...	878,940,000	...	710,310,000	...	168,630,000
1860...	975,240,000	...	757,267,000	...	217,973,000
1861...	906,660,000	...	701,406,000	...	205,254,000
	2,760,840,000	...	2,168,983,000	...	591,857,000
1866...	824,130,000	...	664,093,000	...	160,037,000
1867...	859,680,000	...	747,256,000	...	112,424,000
1868...	886,860,000	...	779,397,000	...	107,463,000
	2,570,670,000	...	2,190,746,000	...	379,924,000

From the preceding tables, which include yarns, it will be seen that the quantity of cleaned cotton taken for goods exported exceeds, in 1866–7–8, by 21,763,000 lbs., the quantity taken in 1859–60–61; but if we look at the home consumption, we find a decrease of 211,933,000 lbs., or 35 per cent.

The following are the computed values both for the export and home consumption for the years named:

		Value of Exports.		Value of Home Consumption.
1859	......	38,744,000	....	9,198,000
1860	......	42,141,000	....	12,129,000
1861	......	37,579,000	....	10,997,000
		£118,464,000	....	£32,324,000
1866	......	57,903,000	....	13,954,000
1867	......	53,128,000	....	7,993,000
1868	......	50,128,000	....	6,911,000
		£161,159,000	....	£28,858,000

From these tables it will be seen that the money value of cotton goods exported, during the three years named, increased by £42,695,000, but the value of the home consumption was decreased by £3,466,000.

From a consideration of the statistics which have been given, we may logically draw the following conclusions:—

1. That the common belief that our trade is being supplanted by continental manufacturers is all a delusion, inasmuch as our exports to the continent have materially increased, whilst the imports to us from the continent have decreased.
2. That as our exports of cotton goods during the past three years have been greater than ever before, it follows that the world will take large quantities of cotton goods even at high prices.
3. That the main if not the only cause of the great depression which has existed in the cotton trade, has arisen from the falling off in the home trade.

At all times, and more especially so when there is any dearth of the raw material, be it cotton or anything else, a good home demand will always ensure a better and more profitable trade than the same foreign demand would do, because we have then this advantage over all competitors—we are independent of tariffs, we have our market on the spot, whereas they have to pay to get to it, and whatever the amount be that the transit of goods cost, by so much have we the advantage over them. But when much of the demand comes from those countries that are our competitors in manufacturing industry, then it is plain that the case is reversed. They have the market on the spot, and we have to pay to get to it, and other things being equal, whatever the cost of transit to their market may be, by so much will they have the advantage over us; and as there is not cotton enough to keep both their mills and ours running, they will outbid us, and keep their mills going, and we must get along as we can. Had our home trade, instead of falling off 35 per cent, increased as the continental trade has done, then we should have competed with them upon equal terms. Unfortunately, however, we have first had to bid against them for the cotton, and then, in order to keep our mills going, we have had further to bid against them in their own markets for cloth, which has entailed upon us long-continued and most severe losses.

During the American War, the uncertainty in regard to its continuance, and the general fear that, when it ended, there would be at once from three to four million bales of cotton liberated, prevented capitalists from investing their money in promoting the growth of cotton. Since the war terminated, the gloomy dulness that has continually hung over the Manchester market, and the utter impossibility of doing business except at a heavy loss, and then only when helped by a spurt in the Liverpool cotton market, has knocked all heart out of capitalists, and prevented them latterly from embarking in the culture of cotton. Now, had we had a good demand for cotton goods, it would have dispelled the gloomy feeling that has hung over Manchester all the last three years; it would have relieved the market of goods, and prevented those heavy shipments which have so glutted foreign markets, and which have proved so disastrous to shippers; prices in foreign ports, as a consequence, would have been higher, and we should have had a healthier and more reliable trade; a good home demand, therefore, would first have given more profit to the manufacturer, and then, by relieving foreign markets, would also have saved the merchant from his heavy losses. It would, moreover, by inspiring confidence, have stimulated the growth of cotton, and in every way, therefore, would have given us help, and speeded on the time when we should secure a full supply of the raw material.

A moment's reflection will make it clear to the

thoughtful mind, that the reduced home demand for cotton goods must arise from one of two causes,—either we, as a nation, spend our money on other things, or we are become poorer, and have not the money to spend.

It is very commonly said that, in consequence of the increased cost of cotton goods, people cannot afford to pay the prices for them, and hence their use has been superseded by woollen, linen, &c. If people were universally well clad this answer might be deemed satisfactory, but, in the presence of the millions of our ragged countrymen, who stand sorely in need of a new shirt, or an additional sheet to their beds, the answer is simply absurd.

We are the richest nation in the world, and yet a great portion of our population are in rags. Why is this? Is it because they get insufficient wages, and are therefore poor? No, it is because they squander their earnings in intoxicating drinks. Let us look how far this assertion is borne out by facts.

For the three years ending with 1868 the expenditure upon intoxicating drinks in the United Kingdom was as follows:—

1866	£101,252,551
1867	99,900,502
1868	102,886,280
	£304,039,333

Here is an astounding fact: in three years we spend on intoxicating drinks £304,039,333, and yet, upon cotton goods, our staple production, we spend only £28,858,000. Taking the population of the United Kingdom at thirty millions, it gives for each man, woman, and child, for the three years, £10. 2s. 6d. for drink, and 19s. 6d. for cotton goods; or, taking the year 1868, we get £3. 8s. 7¾d. per head for drink, and 4s. 7¼d. for cotton. Taking a family of five persons, we have £1. 3s. 0¼d. spent on cotton, and £17. 3s. 2¾d. on intoxicating liquors.

The question as to the utility of alcoholic liquors as beverages is one that I believe science and experience have decided in favour of the total abstainer; but, apart altogether from that question, and admitting the statement, as to the good of these drinks, to be all that is said, there is no sane person who will plead for the spending one hundred millions per annum on intoxicating drinks. One-fourth of this amount would be amply sufficient to satisfy any reasonable requirements; and, therefore, we may safely say that at least seventy-five million pounds of this amount might be saved. If this were appropriated to the purchase of manufactured and useful articles, it would give such an impetus to trade as has never been known. Ten millions of it applied to purchasing cotton goods would at once more than double our home trade, and place us in such a position as would banish all complaint of bad trade.

I am aware that with the present dearth of cotton we could never have a thoroughly steady and healthy trade; but, as I have shown, we should, even under these circumstances, be far better off than we are at present, because (1st) we should be far richer, and better able to bid for cotton in the market of the world, more of it would consequently come to our mills; and (2nd) our workpeople, were they sober, would be able to put up with short time without inconvenience; we might thus, with comfort to all, regulate the consumption to the supply, and secure a far more profitable and a steadier trade than we now enjoy.

The different ways in which the enormous expenditure on intoxicating drinks injures our trade are too numerous to particularise, but I will point out three or four.

1st. Its influence on the labour market. To illustrate this I will state a fact. In the *Scotsman* newspaper for January 2nd, 1869, there is a description of the Caledonian distillery at Edinburgh. In this distillery, we learn 40,000 gallons of spirits are manufactured weekly, or 2,000,000 per annum. At 16s. per gallon, this would be over £1,500,000; the quantity of grain consumed is 800,000 bushels; the number of men employed is stated to be 150.

Now, if this £1,500,000 were spent upon manufactured goods, or in building houses, or draining waste lands, it would give employment to from 12,000 to 15,000 persons or more, and if the whole sum spent in intoxicating drinks were appropriated, it would find work for at least 1,200,000 more people than are at present engaged. Here, then, is an answer to the question, What shall be done with our surplus population? Not send them as emigrants to other countries, but by spending our money judiciously we should find them abundant work at home; we should have work for all and to spare.

Strange! marvellously strange! that men of intelligence cannot see this. They go on forming emigration societies, sending our best workmen,—who above all others should stay at home,—out of the country, and housing in workhouses and gaols a whole host of paupers and criminals. If three-fourths of the money spent on intoxicating liquors were spent on clothing, furniture, and in the erection of houses, &c., it would find full employment for all our emigrants and able-bodied paupers, and besides this, pauperism itself and crime would fast disappear, and all those perplexing problems of our legislation, which are a disgrace to our Christianity and our civilisation, would be solved, and many of the evils over which we have so bitterly to mourn, would be eradicated.

Another way in which it injures our trade is, that it increases our imports and lessens our exports. The author of a tract, entitled "An Enquiry into the Commercial Position of Great Britain," which has been widely circulated in Manchester, makes a great point of this, and tries to father it upon our free-trade policy; but, if it were not for the wines, spirits, grain, and sugar we import, in consequence of what we destroy in brewing and distillation, our imports would be very much lessened, and reduced pretty nearly to the value of our exports; and the money now paid to foreign countries for these articles would be laid out upon our own home trade, thus accumulating our riches and stimulating our manufactures, and finding employment for our artisans.

Another way in which the liquor traffic injures trade is, that it seriously augments our local taxation. The expenditure of the United Kingdom, under the head of poor's rates and police rates, for the last three years, is as follows :—

	England & Wales.	Scotland.	Ireland.
1866...........	£9,989,121	£796,574	£759,174
1867...........	10,905,173	830,279	756,046
1868...........	11,380,596	842,893	848,971
	£32,274,890	£2,469,746	£2,364,191

Adding all these figures together, we get a grand total of £37,108,827 ; or, to take another view of the question, we have paid more for poor's and police rates during the last three years, by £8,000,000, than the entire value of our home consumption of cotton goods. If it had not been for the liquor traffic, the thirty-seven millions need not, at the outside, have been above seventeen, and the other twenty millions would have been available for our trade; if it had been used in the purchase of cotton goods we should not to-day have been in the deplorable condition we are.

I have often heard it stated, and there is considerable truth in the statement, that owing to the heavy local taxation on Manchester and other large towns, spinners and manufacturers find it impossible to compete with country mills where the taxation is lighter; and hence it is observed that whilst no new mills are being built in Manchester, &c., old mills are being stopped, and the trade is gradually shifting to lighter taxed regions.

What is true of districts in the same country is equally true of different countries; the rates which a manufacturer has to pay must come out of trade profits, and this makes the production of goods more expensive; and, consequently, other things being equal, if a large mill be taxed at the rate of £500 per annum in this country, but only £100 on the continent, then the continental manufacturer has an advantage of £400 per annum over his English competitor.

Another way in which the liquor traffic seriously injures our trade is, that it causes food to be dearer. In 1868, 52,669,089 bushels of malt were used in brewing and distillation, besides other things. This would make at least 1,000,000,000 4lb. loaves, or nearly four loaves per week for every family in the United Kingdom.

Writers on trade and commerce always argue (and rightly so) that a bad harvest causes dear food, and leads to bad trade, because people having more to pay for food cannot afford clothing; but, so far as the result goes, there is no difference between 50,000,000 bushels of grain destroyed by bad weather and 50,000,000 destroyed by distillation; in both cases the food is abstracted from the market, and causes prices to rise; and in the latter case, in addition to the destruction of the grain, there is the destruction of the people's morality, and burdens and evils entailed too numerous to enumerate.

'Tis clear, therefore, that if the grain which is used in brewing and distillation were used in baking, we should have a far more plentiful supply; it would, therefore, be cheaper, and as a consequence, people, having less to spend on food, would have more for clothing; our trade would therefore be augmented. Thus, in a multitude of ways, it is clear that our present bad trade arises not from a bad foreign demand, but from a deficient home trade, which is entirely the result of our squandering our money upon things not only useless, but things which are pernicious, and which in all their subsequent relations and results continue to injure our trade and commerce, and also to demoralise our population.

It is a common observation on 'Change that prices of cotton goods are too high; that people cannot afford to pay them. During 1868 prices were not 20 per cent dearer than before the war, the entire extra cost being less than £1,500,000 sterling, or about 11½d. per head for our entire population. If we are got to such a pitiable state that an extra 11½d. per head per annum stops trade, we are certainly in a sad plight, especially when at the same time we are spending annually over £3 per head on liquors that result in demoralisation and misery heart-rending to contemplate.

It may be said that people were as given to drunkenness before the present depression in trade as they are now. This is true only in degree, for the evil has yearly grown worse, and the point is sure to be arrived at when the strain can no longer be borne. The invention of the steam engine, the loom, the spinning jenny, and other valuable machines placed in our hands for a considerable time a monopoly of wealth; our coal fields, iron mines, &c., supplemented these; and had we been wise, and during the last fifty years have properly husbanded and used the wealth thus placed within our reach, we should to-day have been free from the fearful pauperism that marks us out as a disgrace among the nations of the earth. The burden of crime, pauperism, and demoralisation that results from the liquor traffic, every day becomes more and more oppressive; and the time is fast hastening when, if we do not grapple with the evil, we shall sink beneath its weight, and take our place in the second or third rank among the nations of the earth. Persia, Babylon, Carthage, Rome, and other kingdoms, which once were in the front rank, have played their part, and now are scarcely known except in history. It was their profligacy and debauchery which sunk them, and will sink us, not only commercially, but morally and religiously, unless we adopt means to bring it in check.

The remedy for our bad trade then lies entirely with ourselves. If we think we can continue to squander one hundred millions yearly on drink, and by the spending thereof increase very materially our local taxation, and sap the foundations of industry, virtue, and morality, we shall be greatly mistaken.

We may have an abundant and profitable trade; we may have a contented, virtuous, and happy people; but if we are ever to secure this, we must remove the temptations to intemperance which are planted broadcast over the land.

In this argument I have taken no account of the domestic, social, and moral evils which result from intemperance. I have written as a commercial man; and I appeal to the manufacturers of Lancashire and of the United Kingdom generally, to consider the question thus imperfectly put before them; and if only a tithe of what I say be true, it will furnish abundant cause for immediate reform in a system so fraught with evil as the liquor traffic.

A. Ireland & Co., Printers, Manchester.

www.ingramcontent.com/pod-product-compliance
Lightning Source LLC
LaVergne TN
LVHW011146110826
845150LV00008B/2537

9781418192198